MW01101539

GOOD RIVER

GOOD RIVER
POEMS BY SARA VANDER ZWAAG

Good River by Sara Vander Zwaag

Copyright © 2020, Sara Vander Zwaag

All Rights Reserved.
Printed in the United States of America.

Front & Back Cover Photos: Caroline O'Connor Thomas
Cover Design: KT Gutting
Editors: Courtney Jameson & KT Gutting

First Edition Book
978-1-7323992-7-3

Published by White Stag Publishing LLC
www.whitestagpublishing.com

For Tyler

and

For Dr. Slome

*"The heart wants
her horses back."*

-Ada Limón

DEAR CAMERON,

Today the light finally turned
into that September kind: so much
more orange at the sky-tilt. We resume
taking smoke into our bodies, fire
crusted on our coast like resin
in the bowl and a hurricane calling
dibs on the other shore. Did you cry on the plane?
The night before you left, eight of us gathered
on the balcony of an empty bar.
We put glass against our mouths and watched
four planets undress in a too-perfect
curve. I knew it was Mars right away, knelt
deeply to the slight red. Fernet-sharp
teeth proclaimed the night was bless*ed*.
There was not a single lie said. The planets
were really there. We toasted to knowing
the memory of anger, rare, making you stay
for a cigarette thrown on a couch.
Today, I already miss you. I go outside
to buy spinach. In the parking lot,
a truck's only bumper sticker urges,
"Lay down in the light."

RUSSIAN RIVER

                                               Sunlight heaps the river, not yet burned

Saturdays are new to us. We unfairly claim

                                               a sunken tree. We decide it's perfect

At the shore, a child commands

                                               his father: *"Tell me what I'm most afraid of!"*

Two canoes pass with men and women

                                               spitting from the confines of their vessels

from the two-ness of the running water

                                               They shout: *"Don't tell me what to do—I know how*

to paddle!" Parts of the tree roots turn to stone

                                               seem to stiffen and gnarl into calm footholds

A place to hang our hats, floaties shaped

                                               like donuts and gummy bears, sunglasses, a beer

The tree provides a precipice, oaky volume

                                               reflects our adequacy. Love not placed in a canoe

breath not held. Later we will scramble up

                                             the concrete edge of a bridge and I'll be unusually

brave. Later we will place frozen

                           kitchen towels along my radiating body

bring the fever down, let the sun out

                           To enter the night not gilded into a star by

the absence of water and shade

                           "*I'll be okay,*" I promise. "*Go to sleep*"

PSYCHOANALYSIS

Today,
as an astronaut inside her suit
inside her fiery vessel,
as the stern post-noon
degree of Autumn light
through a tree belatedly reveals
orange fruits hanging in the leaves
which I can't name but which might be
persimmons, I feel okay. Soft
to myself, what's outside.
What's between the caverns of bone, nose,
brain, and eye—warm and velvet as though
a bit of me is napping there, in a light-beam,
underneath some table or chair.
As though on the perfect high
from a butane flame wicked against
the perfect plant: not tired, not awake,
ever-so-slightly dulled enough to feel
lovely and still of breath. To go through
the world all canals and underwater,
like the Klonopin used to induce, gently
drugging me to sleep each afternoon.
Sweet pilly godmother of molasses
cloaking my body with weight.
Today, this happened
on its own.
Yesterday, a coworker brought me bread.
Yeasty and vegan, the dust of flour
blew a gentle heavenly carb smell into my
hands and the car and the cutting board.
I tore it to pieces and mixed it around
with squash that dissolved when I bit it
and peppers that shrank in the oven-heat,

4

olive oil, onion. Maybe the bread
begat this beautiful state.
I'm about to eat more for lunch.
My dad said on the phone three years ago
it's not will things be okay, it's that
they already are: the sandwich and I,
the light, and the softness of which I can't
pinpoint a source but swim in, today, gladly.

JUNE WEDDINGS

I let myself out
of control
again; I became a river
of wine. I ate cupcakes
made with butter.
We danced, and I was
the back of the grind.
I drove home unready,
essentially blind,
shared alkaline food
with the girl I gave
a ride. The highway
went by as far as I knew.
I was just like my family
that night. Unloosed
my bladder on the poor,
empty sidewalk, blocks shy
of my toilet, silk pulled
in fistfuls hurriedly
up my thighs.

IT WAS SO FUCKING GREEN

And we jumped
into it. From plane
to neon. Lucifer
headlong unto
the lush
mounds, from heaven
to heaven. If one
falls through
the sky,
here then one
arrives. This time,
it was real
falling, green
to gather the bodies.
Life! To land on,
to fly into, prostrate,
face west, face
God, feet alight,
no knees
askew—heaven
the color, not
the place. *Holy*
is living
through it,
one foot on the side
of a plane,
waiting. Fixate
on the distance.
The angel doesn't want
to leave until it does,
then we begin
in earnest: god-made,
God's hand.

Both/and. The ground
is coming, is here.

OLD PARABLE: VINEYARD AND VINE

I'll wrap you up
in a bottle of red

swaddle you
with tannins and red teeth

chisel into your belly
with laughter's pick-axe

eat all your crackers
take bites of your chocolate

ask you how the visit was
ask you for water

look at pictures of puppies
feel at home in your home

take away your breath with the mirth
of a meeting for the toilet-traveled

and raise my hand
as I did then

to your glee
to the trophy and trouble

DEAR CAMERON,

All Sunday, scavenger
birds circled the pines
across the street,
almost brazenly—
their number so great
against the lazy traffic.
You asked if I would
turn my body
into flame and ash.
Would the birds take
death by smoke
as well? Would we linger
longer in air than soil?
Everything ended
in America Saturday.
The votes clanged out
no remorseful fucks.
The carrion-eaters
flew around trees eagerly.
Half of half of us
croaked an ancient dirge
to our own dead selves—
have tasted our blood
gushing from a cut lip
and found bruises
in the shower—
to remember later
how young.
This is nothing against
the repurpose of a body
decayed. But we put shells
on the windowsill
of the apartment. But we

toss, ungoverned, in sleep.

CAMP FIRE* (THE SUN WANTS ME TO LOOK)

All day we poured crushed rock and water,
stones you can lick, and sand.　　　We finally found
that suitable dresser and pushed it neatly into place
along with a free couch and the door love built

to keep us,　　　fondly, apart. In the evening, we sat in bed
split with the cat we call baby, mending many holes
with a purple childhood sewing kit; its bottom bejeweled
with ancestor's buttons, broken scissors in the face of a crane.

All day we made the apartment shift form
and pressed prayer petals　　　into its bedrock. Gave it time
to digest our new design. We sewed neat lines
side-by-side, watched *Parenthood*, cried.

Love will watch our tears and make
quartz from the salt, which we remember to buy
with iodine. Love forgave me　　　burning rice
and brushed the hair from our arid faces. So here it is:

outside, the ground burns. Leagues of trees & fields afire.
We cover our mouths to protect our chests.　　　Gunshots sing
the fire's wedding bells: it's burning from both sides
toward something: our union, our wheat and hearth.

Swarms of black birds fly off into the lilac smoke.
It's only just now cold enough to wear a coat, but that doesn't matter
to the fire. Wind and water's ghosting, thousands of cars on highways
driving south and out,　　　making future fires for our children to flee.

*Butte California, November 8th. 2018. The deadliest wildfire in California history.

ON A TUESDAY IN FEBRUARY, A MARS ROVER DIED

On Mars, Opportunity clicked off
its final report.

On a sidewalk in Berkeley, we found
an enormous, impractical mirror.

The moon that night
was so huge and reflective

we thought it might be a god's
swollen eye, peering at us

with immense vulnerability.
Do the rovers know they were made to end

in soft, dirt-mound coffins? Solar panels
losing their sight to more and more sand.

We take what they have beamed:
postcards of beautiful numbers.

We could rebirth the dirt with data.
Two days from now, a best friend

will move to New Zealand.
We fret and relent in the lead-up:

the unending ramp toward whatever
is happening next. The digging site

on which we pour anxiety's concrete
but never build frames.

When it happens, it's never as bad.
That's the secret. The balloons

in our chests continue inflating,
and we eat as much as we can stomach.

We put our faces in margaritas: blood
oranges from the winter market,

salt from the Safeway.
On Mars, the rovers roll on dusty tires,

claiming acres for plots
in which nothing will grow. Time

is entirely different, though barely.

We may not be the "rose" kind

so pleasing, even as they curl
into gross versions

of women, but we love the smell,
and still the lilies next to us remain

of what they were last Thursday.
When it happened, it wasn't so bad.

SKINNY-DIPPING (WHEN THE MAN IN THE FISHING BOAT LINGERS)

The river wanted me
buck-ass nude   Bright as the sun
on my thighmeat, perfectly cold

Deep knowing made me
a wise, naked monk   I held up a patient
finger, waited for a friend and a bottle of wine
The wind made the river flow

opposite the current   Euphoria was there
for us, bare as we dared to be
A bikini makes a goddamn difference

Somehow the cold and the river-worms
+ wine + daylight + dear god, are we alone
all stammered *My! Body!*
Bellowed *Get the hell gone!*

I belonged to me and the circling hawks
determined to stalk the redwoods
until they found what beckoned below

Strings of muscle and fur so worth
an hour's hunt   As though in secret collusion
as though just as nearly birds
from their berth their wingspans

their knifing beaks
arose from the distance a series of boats
full of men and their castles

We barely made it out in time
to fling ourselves onto the dock, cover

15

                              our nipples, cast a quick prayer
                              to the earth mother and blend to the rotting wood

I turned and said *pretend we're dead*
but my friend couldn't comprehend
didn't hear the river's siren didn't see
the haunting birds didn't lose her body once before

                              One boat remained: a fisherman
                              lone in a tipped-back boat, casting
                              too close to the shore, caught

on some rock-form or tree-root
so convenient, so close to us, scented, made of skin
The dock might be flesh   The dock is
our mother's body keeping us warm

ON THE FIRST DAY OF DECEMBER, THE LORD CREATED PONY RIDES

The children of our neighborhood clung
like flies to sticky ribbon on every facet of the holiday festival—
tiny Silas, Mason, and Grier found a way to tag
all the store's toys with fingerprints while their parents were off
buying latkes and coffee, eating as clouds of heat
puffed from their hands, flanked by mounds of fake snow

and a tent full of homespun bunny-ear headbands.
The worst part was the ponies, chained
to the spokes of a cruel circle: the opposite of an open plain,
a creature you'll never out-run. The smell of their shit
and hay pressed into the lines of the parking lot.
I looked them in the face as though it was brave of me.

I counted the number of toddlers learning
to disregard the animals they gleefully clenched.
Their parents took enough pictures to paper a stall.
Do you know what I saw when I looked at their faces?
Nothing. Hard quiet. It was difficult, even impossible,
to find their eyes underneath the soft hair of their foreheads.

GIFT

We need a new dresser
for the apartment.
The dresser there now
is honestly heinous,
its edges and gaps packed
full of rat shit,
its flat belly stained
with urine. They lived inside
for more months than I'd like
to admit. The cursed furniture
came without handles
and a mirror to be remounted
on the marble top.
Ben and I drove two hours
to his family friend's dead
brother's place. We also took
an orchid I later killed
and a gold-painted frame
I've never unboxed.
The new dresser will be trusty:
hold the TV with vigor and grace.
We already found two
free vestiges—walnut-soft,
gently nicked—left on the shoulders
of Sebastopol and Oakland
as if California *knew* somehow.
They were too big
but otherwise perfect.
Time folds and shimmers
in that spot in the corner.
The years' creased chiffon
bundles and glows
as though I could reach through

and pet myself back then,
quietly waiting on the bed
to be made alive.

HISTORY OF MY APARTMENT

my sister found it

Ben moved in

Ben moved out

then I

rats

rats for fucking ever

me

me and Tyler

DEAR CAMERON,

I think a lot about using my hand
to hold onto something,
like my other hand. As a kid waiting
in line for a roller coaster,
my Dad told me colors
don't exist for real: what's blue
to me might be for you
a tiny darting fish.
I was terrified.

Like a lake's edge
bowed with petal-full narcissus.
A mirror exercise plied by surprise.
The days fill with mold
and our bodies hack back
that plume of miniscule life.
Is it wet where you are?
Have the chimes of church on Sunday
meant a great deal to a hair-width
of your memory? Thick like wind atop you.

I get that way. I ate four handfuls
of trail mix at a party and watched full adults
throw dirty ping pong balls
into nonexistence. How large is God
in that waiting cup? The void
where the balls roll downhill forever.
The future might be an old friend
asking us to stay for dinner,
a cup of mulled wine or handful
of wildflowers. Pop rocks
in the sun. It might be beautiful
where we keep going.

June Weddings

A field held in a cup of trees,
green to keep your hands. Birds ring
through the trees above the altar,
the heads of those betrothed.
When you return to Pennsylvania
in the summer, unencumbered,
so unlike the gray-white
of January, something unlocks
a memory of place. What is worthy
of loving or telephoning back:
Regretfully, I have ignored
your beauty; I am thusly
at the service of your forests.
Mosquitoes flock to perfume
and silk-stifled skin, your sample-sized
musk-honey arrogance. An announcement
of presence we call irritating, but really,
no hairs to press apart: it's here,
we are too, so are they.

ANOTHER WAY TO SAY I'M HERE

When you open the door
the world blows open.

Your niece isn't your niece
by blood, but she's crying:

full hot springs from face
to bedspread, saltwater

so familiar you can taste it.
In the doorway, you touch that

scalloped edge of fear, because
it's there for you to explore

like the surprisingly electric
world beneath tooth enamel

only known to those who've
broken in—you couldn't stop

reaching your tongue to stroke
the wild sparkles, a bit of pain

worth discovering. Two seconds
in the doorway and you know no

immediate sounds to make
but go to the bed to lie with her

and touch her face and tell her
your body is a real body

and she can hold it
however she needs.

NEW PATTERN DEVELOPMENT

Hold the sound
jewel-tone
under your tongue
and walk
across the street
the way you never go.
There, they fence
the houses differently.
Just a day later
the stretchy synthetic webs
and caving gourds
congregating
with abandoned candies
seem so out of place.
It's also the sunshine,
the way summer bleeds
into November,
the wildfires,
the heat.

THE MEMBRANE HAD A DOOR THE WHOLE TIME

(Before therapy: I loved others like a suffocating glue.)

23, Fisherman's Wharf: convinced a palm reader
to observe my right hand* for free.

A metaphor: a heart filled with blood—
the membrane that protects from life's prodding harshness.

To survive: I pretend as though everything's normal and chill,
even though a god-sworn miracle loops with ridiculous joy around my body, constantly.

The person I love: puts on costumes to please me. I intend to laugh
but instead cry with thunderous precision.

I wonder: if this is what Joan of Arc felt when she touched the cerebral pulse
of holiness. A percentage of light known to few and ultra matter.

For a second there: I felt it all at once.

*My palm said I wasted my life trying to make people love me. My palm said I didn't know what to do
with love: do you put it in a drawer? Do you water it every day? I believed whatever idea of me
anyone had: their guess was as good as mine. My palm said I would get it back someday, what I gave
away too freely.

SIMPLE LOVE POEM
for Tyler

Would that I could   be like the water
in which your body   refracts, amazes me.
That moment when   you're swimming down
to give me room,   I love you then
as the octopus opening   its jar,
which is to say,   I just know how to.
You would be the water   in my cup
should I drink,   and you would be
the water standing by   as we float.

GOLDEN HOUR

A bend in the Russian River,

the middle of the end

of a decade.

We're failing with dignity,

making our way

from one slippery shore

to another.

Our last days of vitality—

our youth

tethered out near-distantly—

arms greased

and bearing weight well.

We're creating a home here:

the gap where two bodies

make new circles

for shared carousel horses to run.

The dragonflies arrive

to replace the flies and water-worms.

Ghastly clouds

of milling bodies

sticker and hole-punch the sun.

Remember when the air

was all gnat fields

thick as thighs

sewn together in the heat?

Popsicle-stains begging

the swarm toward your face.

Open, helpless.

Now, the cold water

asks forgiveness.

You'll forget

as soon as it happens,

as it's happening,

as it passes, are you there

DEAR CAMERON,

It's quiet here.
I didn't notice
before. I drove in
to campus
and by god
beheld your face
smiling on a banner
of scholarship.
Abrupt but
in-violently,
I thought, "my friend!"
and drove on.
I thought your face
will never age,
and I may not see
its flesh for who knows
how long, but
here you are
on the flags,
on the holy grounds
of the academy
where the birds
and baseball bats
are trellising
a tepid hymn
of chimes.

HIGHWAY 1

Blooms into a cliff. This time,

I'm not afraid of sitting

in the passenger seat—the better

view, the side tracing asphalt grooves

along a blue-white ocean seam.

We go there and back by accident

at the same golden time.

I don't say it's God here, but I think so.

Not heaven like large men

in sandals, long beards gilded

for festivals of souls dancing

to the bass of distant stellar waves.

But maybe a piece of cake, a friend's hand.

And on this road / in this car

/ at this campsite where I start the fire

and we zip ourselves into rocks

worn away by an ever-cold pacific edge,

I think heaven is the right word,

and I try to sit still.

EVERYTHING WILL BE FINE

We're already there. The next day waits for me to serve breakfast in a blue dish. We re-arrange the apartment to match my therapist's yellow den. It's unintentional, perfect this way. We have a constant supply of cooked grains to shovel into Tupperware and then our mouths. The animal is never without a lap. We're already inside the future I imagined would never break its yolk on my waiting head. Holy fuck, we're putting records on the player and bouncing back and forth between two TVs to make sure we never miss a single glittering fist of confetti. The animal has four hands to feed it, gladder and fatter with every day. We might love nothing more than one another, constantly raising our hands to join each other's team. With pride wear the green pinny, with holes and eternal stank. Jog across the field, slip in the slick muddy grass, fall, shake your body laughing, put another hole in the pinny, repeat the next day, forever, etc.

JUNE WEDDINGS

In a town small enough
to be half family, we found
the Mississippi sidelong cornfields,
an everlasting sort of beige.
We took pictures as a group
in front of the river, held hands
in twos, shouted "kiss your bride!"
Kiss your bride.

THE SMALLER ISLAND

The island coast folds in on itself and constantly drinks
from the raincloud

Clementine skin like flesh   sandwiches made of bread and sprouts

The equatorial sun is exacting
the way a train track is exacting

It beats
          a gleeful contour
on the rippled hills
          It bludgeons our bodies
               into pink marbles

Spread me out and open
over the prime meridian
                         or the equator

A thousand wings and filaments
                    a single white hair
on the side of the face

Magnolias freckle the branches
and the branches scratch

          Small citruses cleaved of their chapels
          silver reengaging the skin

We have found the painting

          In the painting are whale sounds but not rendered
Each decision could be wrong
and on the trail marker

arrows could mean go either way

      One way really to the waterfall   but we go there last

BLUE, MICHIGAN

This splintered state can keep me

in a lake so cold so saltless

we find ourselves a little less beheld;

so many limbs and pool noodles

spend themselves returning

to an ever-drifting boat.

The blue crops up around us

on the drive home. Here,

too, I can think of no other

body to be in.

How new this feels; love

allows me to.

On the balcony, my body

puffs like a blue flower, all stem

and head, and we think almost

everyone has heard us,

and that's okay.

In the water, it's sapphire

skin and the equal gems

of a newly-wedded friend.

We came so far to eat

for her; to jump from her boat

and later drive away—have I remembered

correctly that blue flowers are

~~least likely~~ most rare?

ACKNOWLEDGMENTS

Firstly, I must thank KT DeBruhl and Courtney Jameson for supporting my work and providing me with incredible opportunities. I'm so grateful to the both of you.

This collection would not have come together without the help of Madeline Gilmore, Cameron Stuart, and Carrie Markowski. Your edits, emails, texts, and love helped me compose and revise these poems, and your writing has inspired me to no end.

To Samantha Niedzielski: are there words? These poems wouldn't be here without you. Thank you for the thousand edits, handwritten notes, hugs of support, almond butter toasts, and cups of coffee.

To Matthew Zapruder: thank you for encouraging me not to give up on myself. Your support prompted me to write and improve most of this collection, for which I am grateful. To my other teachers, particularly Brent Armendinger and Brenda Hillman: thank you for every bit of knowledge you've passed on. Thank you for your poems. I'm so privileged to have learned from you.

To Tyler Hurlburt, Anna Evashevski, Hunter Vander Zwaag, and Dr. Slome: thank you for your love. To my parents: thank you for believing in me and always encouraging me to offer myself to the world with creativity. I love you.

Everything Will Be Fine and *Dear Cameron (1)* were previously published in Issue 1 of Volume Poetry.

Finally, a huge thank you to Caroline O'Conner Thomas for the beautiful artwork used for the front and back covers.

WHITE STAG